RHINOCEROSES

A TRUE BOOK

by

Melissa Stewart

Children's Press®
A Division of Scholastic Inc.

New York Toronto London Auckland Sydney
Mexico City New Delhi Hong Kong
Danbury, Connecticut

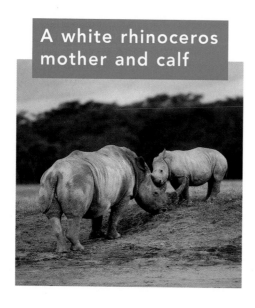

A white rhinoceros
mother and calf

Reading Consultant
Nanci R. Vargus, Ed.D.
Teacher in Residence
University of Indianapolis
Indianapolis, Indiana

Content Consultant
Kathy Carlstead, Ph.D.
Honolulu Zoo

Dedication:
To Colin Campbell Stewart

Library of Congress Cataloging-in-Publication Data

Stewart, Melissa.
    Rhinoceroses / by Melissa Stewart.
        p. cm. — (A True book)
    Includes bibliographical references and index.
    ISBN 0-516-22201-5 (lib. bdg.)   0-516-26992-5 (pbk.)
    1. Rhinoceroses—Juvenile literature. [1. Rhinoceroses.] I. Title.
II.Series.
QL737.U63 S74 2002
599.66'8—dc21   2001017182

Contents

Black rhinoceroses
have two horns.

The Horned Giant

What's the first thing you notice when you look at a rhinoceros? It's probably the horn on its nose. You aren't the only one. The name *rhinoceros* comes from two Greek words that mean "nose horned." Some kinds of rhinos have one horn, while others have two.

Indian rhinoceroses have one horn.

A rhino's horn is made of the same material as your hair and fingernails. It is so tough that it can poke a hole

through metal. Rhinos use
their heavy-duty horns to jab
one another and to fight lions,
hyenas, and other enemies.

These rhinos are fighting with their horns.

A rhino pulling on a tree with its horn

Horns also come in handy when a rhino wants to pull down branches so that it can munch on some tasty leaves.

A rhino's horn begins to grow when the animal is about 5 weeks old—and it never stops. It grows about 3 inches (8 centimeters) longer every year. Some rhinos have horns taller than you! If a rhino's horn breaks off, it will grow back.

A rhino with a broken horn

All About Rhinos

Rhinos have lived on Earth for about 40 million years. At one time, there were more than thirty kinds of rhinos living in Europe, Asia, Africa, and North America. Today, there are five kinds of rhinos. Three kinds live in Asia, and two kinds live in Africa.

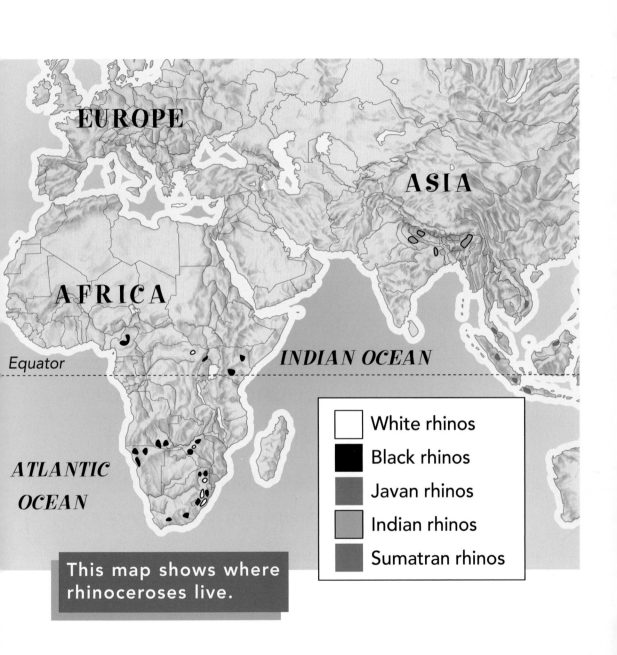

EUROPE

ASIA

AFRICA

Equator

INDIAN OCEAN

ATLANTIC
OCEAN

	White rhinos
	Black rhinos
	Javan rhinos
	Indian rhinos
	Sumatran rhinos

This map shows where rhinoceroses live.

Scientists have found fossils of a 66,000-pound (30,000-kilogram) rhino that lived in Asia millions of years ago. It was the heaviest land animal that ever lived—heavier than any dinosaur. Today, the largest and heaviest animal on land is the elephant. Rhinos and hippos are the next-largest animals.

You might think rhinos, hippos, and elephants are closely related to one another. But rhinos have more in common with horses, zebras, and tapirs.

Rhinos belong to a group of animals that includes horses (left), tapirs (middle), and zebras (right).

Rhinos have three toes on each foot.

All these animals have an odd number of toes on each foot. Horses and zebras have one toe on each foot. A tapir has five toes on each foot. A rhino has three toes on each foot. A thick hoof protects the bottom of each toe. Some people think that a rhino's footprint looks like the ace of clubs in a deck of cards.

Doesn't the bottom of a rhino's foot look like the ace of clubs?

Though they are bulky, rhinos can run quickly over short distances.

Have you ever noticed that a horse gallops high on its toes? That is why it can run so fast. A rhino moves the same way. A huge, bulky rhino is slower than a horse, but it can gallop at a speed of 25 miles (40 kilometers) per hour for short distances.

Horses, zebras, tapirs, and rhinos have other things in common too. They all have teeth that are perfect for crushing and chewing plants. An adult rhino has between twenty-four and thirty-four teeth. It uses them to

All rhinos eat plants.

grind up to 50 pounds (23 kg) of grasses, shrubs, trees, leaves, and fruit every day.

Rhinos also belong to a larger group of animals called mammals. Mice, cats, bears, and people are also mammals. All mammals have a backbone that supports their body and helps them move. They also have lungs and breathe air. They are warm-blooded animals, so their body temperature stays about the same no matter how cold or warm their environment is.

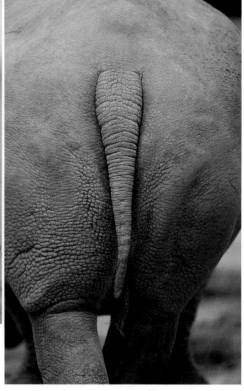

A rhino has hair on its ears (above) and on the end of its tail (right).

One more thing all mammals have in common is hair. You might think that a rhino has no hair, but it does have a little. The hair is on its ears and the tip of its tail. A rhino also has eyelashes.

Baby mammals grow inside their mother until they are ready to be born. When it is time to give birth, a female rhino leaves the group and finds a safe, quiet place. She usually has one baby at a time. A newborn rhino may weigh twenty times more than you did when you were born. In just a few hours, the calf can walk.

When mother and baby return to the group, they keep

A female rhino with her newborn calf

track of each other by mewing quietly. Soon the calf starts to play with other young rhinos. Meanwhile, the females keep an eye out for predators that could attack the calves.

Like all baby mammals, a young rhino drinks mother's milk. Every day, it drinks enough milk to fill twenty glasses. After a few weeks, it starts to eats some solid food. But it continues to drink some milk for up to 2 years.

When a young rhino is about 3 years old, it leaves its mother. A young rhino takes about 5 years to become an adult. Even after it is full grown, a rhino usually waits several more years before it mates and has young of its own. Unless it is injured or killed by hunters, a rhino lives about 30 to 40 years.

Rhinos in Africa

Two kinds of rhinos live in Africa—white rhinos and black rhinos. Don't let these names fool you, though. Both rhinos are really the same color— gray. The white rhinoceros got its name from an Afrikaans word that means "wide." When English-speaking people

White rhinos grazing
in Kenya

heard the word, they thought
it sounded like "white."

Why did the native people
use the word "wide" to
describe this rhino? They were
thinking of its mouth. They
knew that the easiest way to

25

tell the difference between a white rhino and a black rhino is by looking at the animal's mouth.

The white rhino has a wide, square-shaped mouth with broad lips. This kind of mouth is perfect for eating short grasses—the main source of food on the African plains where white rhinos live. The black rhino lives in dense rain forests and dry scrubland. Its pointed upper lip is perfect for grabbing twigs and leaves.

The two kinds of African rhinos also differ in size. White rhinos are larger. Adult male

White rhinos (top) are larger than black rhinos (bottom).

white rhinos may be up to 6 feet (1.8 meters) tall at the shoulder and weigh as much as 7,900 pounds (3,600 kilograms). Adult male black rhinos are about 5 feet (1.5 m) tall at the shoulder and weigh up to 3,100 pounds (1,400 kg). Females are slightly smaller than males.

White rhinos have two horns and usually live in small herds.

White rhinos live in small groups of up to ten animals.

A black rhino sleeping

They rest for most of the day,
and graze in the late afternoon
and at night. Black rhinos also
have two horns, but they usually
live alone. They feed all day long,
and rest at night. Rhinos can
sleep standing up or lying down.

Seeing, Hearing, and Smelling

All rhinos have small eyes and cannot see well, but they have good hearing. They can swivel their ears to pinpoint where a sound is coming from. They also have an excellent sense of smell. They can smell an enemy that is farther away than the length of eight football fields.

A black rhino swiveling its ears

When a male rhino wants to mark off the edge of its territory, it sprays urine and spreads dung with its back feet. Who wouldn't smell that! Females spray urine when they are ready to mate. They also make soft whistling noises.

A male black rhino marking its territory

Rhinos in Asia

Three kinds of rhinos live in Asia—
Javan rhinos, Indian rhinos, and
Sumatran rhinos. These rhinos are
named after the places they live.
African rhinos have no front teeth,
but Asian rhinos do. They use
their sharp, tusk-like front teeth to
slash enemies and other rhinos
that wander into their territory.

A Javan rhino

The Javan rhino looks like it is wearing a suit of armor. The edge of each "armor plate" appears to be marked by a loose fold of skin. This one-horned rhino is extremely rare—only about sixty to eighty survive today. They live in the dense tropical rain forests of Java and South Vietnam. An adult male is about 5.5 feet (1.7 m) tall and weighs close to 4,000 pounds (1,800 kg). A Javan rhino spends most of its time munching on young trees.

Like the Javan rhino, the Indian rhino seems to have a built-in suit of armor. It lives in Nepal and northeast India and prefers swampy areas surrounded by dense elephant grass. An adult male is usually 6 feet (1.8 m) tall at the shoulder and

Indian rhinoceroses

weighs about 4,800 pounds
(2,200 kg). This rhino has only
one horn, but it is very valuable. It may sell for more than
$30,000 per pound ($66,000
per kilogram).

The Indian rhino usually eats
grass and swamp plants. It can

An Indian rhino cooling off in a swamp filled with water plants

fold its lip to one side, making it easier to tear plants out of the ground. The Indian rhino is also a good swimmer. During the hottest part of the day, it enjoys cooling off in a river and eating some water plants. Like other rhinos, the Indian rhino usually stays within a day's walk of water. During droughts, it may use its front teeth to dig for water.

The Sumatran rhino lives in tropical rain forests and along wooded mountain slopes in Sumatra, Borneo, and parts of Malaysia. This very rare rhino is

The Sumatran rhinoceros is sometimes called the "hairy rhinoceros."

easy to recognize. It is smaller than other rhinos, and its body is covered with a shaggy coat of stiff, reddish-brown hairs. Adult males are about 4 feet (1.2 m) tall at the shoulder and weigh about 2,200 pounds (1,000 kg).

In the evening, small groups of Sumatran rhinos feed on tree branches, leaves, and fungi. If a rhino thinks there might be some tasty fruit at the top of a tree, it just plows the tree over to find out. During the day, these two-horned rhinos usually

A Sumatran rhino feeding on plants in a rain forest in Borneo (right) and a Sumatran rhino that has just rolled in the mud (below)

rest in shallow ponds or mud holes. A thick coat of mud protects rhinos from biting insects and the hot sun.

Rhinos in Danger

People have been killing rhinos for thousands of years. To some cultures, a rhino's horn is precious. Some people grind up rhinoceros horn and add it to medicines. Others use it to make knife handles. When European settlers arrived in Africa and Asia, they began to

Rhino horns seized from poachers in Kenya

hunt rhinos and other large animals for sport.

Today only about 12,500 rhinos are left in the wild. About 1,000 more rhinos live in zoos.

It is now illegal to hunt rhinos, but some people do it anyway. This is called poaching. Poachers kill the animal for its valuable horn and its skin. In some national parks, workers cut the horns off rhinos. This might sound cruel, but it can save the animals' lives.

Rhinos are also in danger because their natural habitats are being destroyed. People want to use the land for farms or ranches. Rhinos are an important part of our world, so we must work together to save the horned giant.

As forests in Borneo are cut down (top),
Sumatran rhinos lose their natural habitat.
White rhinos are protected at Lake Nakuru
National Park in Kenya (bottom).

To Find Out More

If you'd like to learn more about rhinoceroses, check out these additional resources:

 **Books**

George, Jean Craig. **Rhino Romp.** Disney, 1998.

Martin, Chryssee Perry. **Russelas: A Rhino in Search of his Horn.** Jacaranda Designs, 1995.

Patent, Dorothy Hinshaw. **Why Mammals Have Fur.** Cobble Hill Books, 1995.

Stewart, Melissa. **Mammals.** Children's Press, 2001.

Theodorou, Rod. **Black Rhino.** Heinemann Library, 2000.

Walker, Sally M. **Rhinos.** Carolrhoda, 1996.

Organizations and Online Sites

African Wildlife Update

4739 Fox Trail Dr. NE
Olympia, Washington
98516
http://www.africanwildlife. org/

This site features up-to-the-minute information about the status of threatened and endangered animals that live in Africa. The black rhino is one of the group's major concerns.

International Rhino Foundation

14000 International Road
Cumberland Ohio 43732
http://www.rhinos-irf.org/

This organization is working to protect rhinos. The site has descriptions and photos of all five kinds of rhinos and maps showing where they live.

International Wildlife Coalition

70 East Falmouth Highway
East Falmouth, MA, USA
02536
http://www.iwc.org

The IWC works to save endangered species and preserve animal habitats and the environment.

KidsGoWild

http://wcs.org/sites/ kidsgowild

This is the kids' page of the Wildlife Conservation Society. It includes wildlife news, wild animal facts, and information on how kids can get involved in saving wild animals and the environment by joining Conservation Kids.

Important Words

calf young of some kinds of mammals, including rhinos

culture group of people that shares the same beliefs, customs, and way of life

drought period of no rain

dung animal droppings

fungi group of plants that includes mushrooms, molds, and rusts

gallop kind of running in which all four feet are sometimes off the ground

habitat place where an animal lives

precious valuable, special

predator animal that hunts and kills other animals for food

territory area where an animal lives, hunts, mates, and raises young

Index

Meet the Author

A few years ago, Melissa Stewart visited the African countries of Kenya and Tanzania. While on safari, she was captivated by rhinos. She saw dozens of them hanging out in waterholes to avoid the hot, midafternoon sun.

Ms. Stewart earned a bachelor's degree in biology from Union College and a master's degree in science and environmental journalism from New York University. She has written more than twenty books for children. Ms. Stewart lives in Marlborough, Massachusetts.